Vygotsky's Children

Vygotsky's Children

Georgetown and Oxbridge Students Meet Urban Youth

John C. Hirsh

With photographs by Harry Mattison

Washington, DC

Copyright © 2017 by John C. Hirsh
New Academia Publishing, 2017

All rights reserved. No part of this book may be reproduced or transmitted in any form or by any means, electronic or mechanical, including photocopying, recording, or by any information storage and retrieval system.

Printed in the United States of America

Library of Congress Control Number: 2017930254
ISBN 978-0-9981477-4-1 paperback (alk. paper)

New Academia Publishing, 4401-A Connecticut Ave. NW, #236,
Washington, DC 20008
info@newacademia.com - www.newacademia.com

Contents

Foreword	vii
Introduction	1
1. Beginnings, and Earlier	9
2. Another Oxford	21
3. Beginning Work	31
4. Apogee	41
5. Concluding?	55
Photo Gallery	63

Foreword

This is an account of four programs in which undergraduates from three universities elected to work with three different groups of young, bright, perceptive, but disadvantaged ethnic minority children, with the intention both of engaging them in academic work, and interesting them in one day attending university.

It is usual in a book like this one to inscribe in the forward the names of those who have advanced the project described, but I have throughout named those whose contributions, many of them far greater than my own, effectively constituted our project. For reasons of privacy I have avoided naming individual students or describing their several accomplishments, which grew and developed during the fifteen years described here. But during that time, as our practices shifted and usually advanced, it was the undergraduate students who undertook to reach our objectives, and it was their work that made the difference. These, as I will show, include both the very many Georgetown students who have taken part in the program I direct at my home university, and those in Oxford and Cambridge, whose programs are the main business of this account, but only some of whom I have known at all well. Otherwise, I record here my indebtedness to colleagues who helped to bring this book about, Charlotte and Mossman Roueché of London, who first suggested it, Carole Sargent, Director of the Office of Scholarly and Literary Publication at Georgetown, and Anna Lawton, founder and Editor of New Academia Press, who nudged it into being. But in deference to their contribution I turn now to Wadham, without which nothing.

During that program's fifteen years, but during the first ten in particular, it was students from Wadham who, working with their lively and perceptive Chaplain, Reverend Doctor Harriet Harris, shaped it, moving away from assisting in what in America would be called the homeroom, to developing, in a mix of freedom and direction, hybrid methods and practices, culminating in the proto-seminars that have proved the most effective for our work. These developments did not come quickly, nor was what developed either predictable or inevitable. The Wadham program grew gradually, with steps backward as well as forward, but even when expectations were frustrated or progress deferred, it was the warmth, heart, and good energy of the Wadham students that taught lessons of acceptance, exchange, and difference that were not in any book. Working together with the children, both sides confronted old assumptions and different cultural values face-to-face, effecting changes and practices not in general use.

All such programs resist perfection, and writing this preface I was reminded of a story concerning the great explorer and scholar Sir Henry Rawlinson, who had once offered a fellow scholar the use, gratis, of some texts he had procured and produced, for use in the man's own work. "I can't possibly use them," the man replied. "There are too many mistakes in them." "I understand," Sir Henry answered. "For you are a scholar, and I am only a pioneer." The Wadham students and their Chaplains were our pioneers, and already, as new programs take shape, others have benefited from what they set out to do. Sadly, the Wadham program now has ended, but it was among the first to address seriously both educational issues and cultural boundaries, all the while drawing upon both friendly interaction and considered intention. So to the excellent students, children and chaplains whose work is here recorded, thank you and congratulations.

Thanks too to the equally fine students of Clare College, Cambridge, also pioneers, who both ventured to a more remote location for their work, and, though starting somewhat later, both led and followed their progressive college towards involvement with the very young, at least for a time. Clare was among the first colleges seriously to embrace Outreach, years earlier, initially tilting toward older children, whose attention it still much invites. And thanks as well to the bright, new students of Magdalene College, Cambridge, who have already improved what they received, and promise well for whatever is to come. All of these, I need hardly add, have both learned and taught.

Throughout this account, short as it is, I have tried to write for both a British and an American audience. Political and cultural challenges in Britain and America differ in many ways, but there are too similarities, some of which may be addressed, as indicated here, by the commitment, energy and enthusiasm of the young. I myself, over the years, have drawn strength, inspiration and ideas from many of them, as I have support from many colleagues, and a certain number of sympathetic administrators. What has connected many of these good people, it seems to me, is that they have thought our work both useful and possibly important, and have understood that it can speak, however imperfectly, both to those who resolve to take part in it, and also, when we do it right, to those whom we mean to serve.

J. C. H.

Introduction

The East End of London, as it is still sometimes called, remains one of the liveliest and most international parts of the city, albeit without the rich variety of cinemas, clubs, museums, office buildings, parks, and through-fares of the more affluent West End, not a handful of city blocks away. King Charles I may have killed a deer here, but it was not among the transformed warehouses, the pubs, restaurants, newsstands, housing projects, the export-import businesses, Toynbee Hall, Spitalfields Market, the Whitechapel Art Gallery, the Bell Foundry, the churches, sidewalk markets, the Royal London Hospital, once the home of the Elephant Man, and the powerful East London Mosque, all of which run along Whitechapel High Street, or stand not far away, in an area formerly associated with Jack the Ripper and the notorious Kraye brothers, now known as Tower Hamlets. Over the centuries the East End has evolved its own rich identity born of those on the margins, Huguenots in the seventeenth century, Irish in the eighteenth, Russian Jews in the nineteenth, Bangladeshi in the twentieth, many of whom, in each century, entered with little, made their mark bravely, and left in triumph. It now belongs to a Bangladeshi community that stands in complex and demanding dialogue with a new Britain.

There are of course other Bangladeshi communities in Britain, but none quite like Tower Hamlets. Some years ago, a Head Teacher whom I was asking for permission to extend to her school a program like one we had already begun in Wapping, warned me, as she said yes, that things in Whitechapel were not necessarily as they were seen from outside of it. It is as though a small town from Bangladeshi has been picked up and set down here, she said.

Things are changing, she added, but at least for now it is possible to be born here, to go to school, get a job, get married, and not feel the need to read and write English. Still, it is a wonderful place. The people understand where they are, and its advantages. You'll be welcome here. And we were.

What follows is an account of how, over fifteen years and not without interruption, first one Oxford college, than two Cambridge colleges, organized and operated two programs in Tower Hamlets, London, in which undergraduate students first taught, then came into seminar-like dialogue with, Bangladeshi and other school children, usually in years five and six – the two years before they leave primary school for secondary. It also notes an interest we took in the early years of secondary, and describes the conversations that took place among persons concerned to bring the programs into being, to consider what effects they were having, and how they might be developed.

A small program, as all the ones recorded here are, can prove a useful testing ground for students and children alike, and although circumstances alter practices, English and American programs can reveal the strengths and limitations of practices brought to bare on mutual challenges, differently resolved. Thus, although lessons learned in one place can indeed inform practices in another, I have written these pages not so much to identify solutions as to suggest what those challenges may be, and to say how, under the different circumstances described here, we sought to address them. As will soon appear, the purpose of the programs changed during the period described. The work of the Oxford and Cambridge students was less to instruct, and not at all to measure, than to reveal, encourage and engage. Their overall mission was to encourage their very young fellow students to understand what a university actually was (not what the word meant), and to do so in such a way that, when the time came, many of them would decide to apply, some, hopefully, to Oxford and Cambridge, but to university in any case.

In educational theory, the word "schema" (*pl.* schemata) designates the way a child constructs his or her world – and many of the children had only a vague idea what a university was, and what went on there. I understand that some will wonder if what the students taught will last. But these children are bright, perceptive and alert. Time will tell, but to many children and in different ways, I have no doubt at all that it will. And what of the students who taught them? Will their schemata be changed as well? And if so how?

The book has five chapters. The first describes generally both the two programs with which it is concerned, and also the program that Georgetown, the university at which I am employed, sponsors at a community known as Sursum Corda, that I have directed for almost thirty years, and that accounts for my interest in urban literacy generally. It also touches upon the academic work, particularly that concerned with whole language teaching strategies that I undertook at Berkeley, and that, together with an interest I took in the work of the Russian psychologist Lev Vygotsky, informed both my thinking in Berkeley, and my subsequent work in Washington. The circumstances surrounding the Georgetown program involved, among other things, aspects of the Washington drug trade, some of them violent, that affected the Sursum Corda community we served, and that contrasted sharply with the world known to most of the Georgetown students who took part in it.

This contrast, together with the events that occurred as our program was taking shape, brought about a degree of cross-cultural communication that sometimes led to understanding and exchange, and that reappeared again in London, as our programs took shape, albeit in very different circumstances. In each case, however, our concern was for introducing the children whom we served to the university, and suggesting what advantages it might have for them in time to come. But this was an understanding that explicitly crossed cultural boundaries, a circumstance that was not lost on some of our left-of-center critics, who assumed, quite mistakenly I believe, that intentionally or not, we regularly privileged "white culture," and, at best, invited our young charges aboard.

The second chapter indicates how I came to be attached to Hermitage School in Tower Hamlets, a state school in Wapping, where I worked among children teaching in what is called the language arts, then understood as reading, writing, listening and talking, and began to explore such social but also cultural difference as I could observe anecdotally, between London and Washington. The comparison brought home to me how powerful such differences can be, and while it is not impossible to address them, they cannot be wished away, nor will good will alone suffice. But it also became possible to consider that the challenges they posed were not insurmountable, and that, as long as advice is taken widely enough, it is possible for something to emerge.

In the third chapter something did emerge, a project in which undergraduates from Wadham College, Oxford, and later on from Clare College, Cambridge, travelled to Tower Hamlets to work in two schools there, with the intention of encouraging children in their work, and no less importantly, in seeing to it that they understood, in some depth, what a university was, and how they could engage it, now and in time to come. The beginnings of the project may have seemed a little uncertain, but was supported (if indirectly) both by circumstances outside of the university, and by persons within it. Oliver Cromwell insisted that a man never rises so high as when he knows not where he is going, but at least we thought we did, and the students in those early days both helped teach the children their lessons and encouraged the idea that, with a little effort perhaps, universities can be breasted by one and all.

Chapter four may indeed represent our program's apogee, which it owed largely to the Head teachers at the schools in which we worked, and also to the Reverend Doctor Harriet Harris, who, together with the Heads, changed its direction in important ways. Even in the early years it became clear it was the idea of a university, not of Oxford in particular, that most needed selling, a circumstance that obtained in programs and projects in other colleges too, notably Pembroke College's excellent program, where to do so was a central commitment. But it became clear too that to have the student act as an assistant teacher hardly emphasized that objective, nor could the Oxford student come regularly or often – though as time went on it appeared that there was something to be said for a degree of irregularity, since when the students appeared they brought with them a change from the ordinary, but one that sprang from more usual occupations. That understanding led to a system of proto-seminars, in which students engaged children in the topics of the hour that they had already taken in hand – Aztecs or Normans, for example – and these proto-seminars could take place either in school or during the return visits the children made to the college, which Harriet Harris had instituted and the children loved.

More recently, Magdalene College, Cambridge, has incorporated a system of question and answer into a program they have begun, which draws upon both the curiosity children have as to what a university is, and also upon the experience of the visiting students themselves. It was during this period as well that a small group of us tried to understand what could be done not only to develop but also to preserve an interest in the university among ethnic minority and disadvantaged children generally, and in the course of things, thanks largely to an experiment that took place at Clare, and was sponsored by Stepney Green Secondary School, we arrived at a three-fold hypothesis concerning the way urban, ethnic minority children may best be introduced to an understanding of the university, one that involved intervention in year 2; year 5 or 6; and years 8 or 9, all of which pointed toward years 11 and 12, which we reserved largely for individual guidance. It was not a conclusion, to be sure, but only the beginning of one, with much left to be proved.

All good things must come to an end, and for that there is chapter five. A new Wadham chaplain had trained as a primary school teacher, and had friends in the profession. Her promise to continue at Hermitage she deferred, and Wadham's students were dispatched instead to help in local schools. But by this time the close connection between the program and the college, and between the program and the SCR, had begun to fade. She kept the dissolution quiet. And no one noticed.

But apart from what was happening in Wadham, the interaction among those who supported the programs, and who actively discussed their role and usefulness had reached a watershed. The experiment begun at Clare needed to continue, but Clare was about to change its Master (though its new one is said to have a like interest in ethnic minority education), and its chaplain, who had done so much to make our discussion and experiment possible, was going to return to Australia. Still, all was not lost. After a brief period in which the connection between Clare and Bigland Green became strained, it resumed again, and now promises very well. If Wadham College really means to terminate its program that would be a pity, but already another Cambridge college, Magdalene College, has become invested in Hermitage, and thanks to a particularly resourceful student, the program has begun. In their first meeting, children and students interacted and worked together with enthusiasm, warmth and evident curiosity, pioneering a practice of Question-and-Answer that promises well for the future. Only that day dawns to which we are awake, Thoreau said. There is more day to dawn. The sun is but a morning star.

1

Beginnings, and Earlier

Oxford and Cambridge Teaching Programs in London—Conditions of Operation in the Beginning—Georgetown University, Sursum Corda and Drugs—Berkeley and Vygotsky—Mottos and Pedagogical Practices

It is more than forty years ago and I am in Oxford talking to a friend in Pembroke College's Middle Common Room, a kind of living room (or sitting room) set aside for the use of graduate students. He is explaining to me, in a northern English accent, why as a schoolboy he didn't want to go to Oxford – which he finally did, however. He is now a graduate student, studying medieval history with Sir Richard Southern as his supervisor. It was too far away and too different, he says. He'd been south before, and didn't like it. But he was smart – "clever" would be the Oxford word -- and first his teachers, then his Headmaster, then all of them and his parents began to pressure him to study for the entrance exam and to apply, which he finally did. But I still remember saying to them, he tells me, that Oxford is where you're made to go if you're English and you're bright. He'd been in Oxford for five years when we spoke, and though he didn't say so, he seemed to me to like it a lot, even though he didn't get on particularly well with Sir Richard (who may not have had his knighthood yet). Cultural differences, he says. He's really very nice, but in some ways we don't connect.

This is an account of two often successful teaching programs, the first begun in Oxford the second in Cambridge, in which students from each university travelled to two state primary schools in Tower Hamlets, London, there to engage the children in a number of curricular and academic topics – the Aztecs, the Normans -- then being discussed by year 5 and year 6 children. The programs were sponsored by the colleges, which initially had encouraged connections that focused upon older children, in years 11 and 12. When the difficulties of those earlier programs became apparent – encouraging applications that could not be accepted when submitted, for example – new ways of proceeding were considered, and in due course adopted, but they made clear as well the necessity of starting the whole process a good deal earlier. Our programs answered that now-understood need, by focusing with some astringency upon encouraging much younger children to understand what a university actually is and has to offer, so addressing the individual child's schema, his or her way of understanding the world. The hope and expectation were that even before the time for application came upon them, the children who took part would begin to understand and accept what was to come. This idea changed and developed over the fifteen years of the program's life, but remained the bedrock of what we sought to accomplish.

In what follows I am not going to discuss, except generally, the persons or the circumstances of those among whom we work, which is their business, not ours. Nor will I linger on the commitment and idealism, much of it evident, of which many of the students who took part gave evidence. To tell the truth, it was not much talked about among themselves – it might have seemed pretentious to have done so – but it was present, occasionally obviously so, as they made time to do what they had promised in a university where it is a simple truth that, in term time at least, everyone is always very busy. Distinctions can be odious, but in Oxford as in Georgetown I have often noticed that students who themselves came from disadvantaged backgrounds were markedly committed to such work, and seemed to feel in it a certain urgency.

But very, very many of the students who took part in such work, whether in Washington or London, and whatever their personal circumstances, did fine work indeed, and reached out to young people whom otherwise they would not have known at all. I am unwilling to say what it meant to them: they were, they are, in most ways like their American colleagues, share their values, attitudes and assumptions, and can and should speak for themselves. But sometimes in Georgetown, when introducing our project to those who were about to join it, I would cite Hillel's three great questions: If I am not for myself, then who will be for me? But if I am only for myself, then what am I? And if not now, when? Very many students would have agreed upon the answers, but all were most welcome to our undertaking. In such matters, students learn from each other best of all.

No doubt my own background needs a word of explanation. A professor of English and American Literature at Georgetown University in Washington, D.C., specializing in late medieval English literature, but also in urban literacy, I received in 1993 a visiting fellowship to Pembroke College, Oxford, which has now become a leader in outreach programs in Oxford, led really quite brilliantly by its Outreach Fellow, Peter Claus. But that distinction was still to come, and when I arrived at Pembroke my primary intention was to read and consult a number of late medieval English devotional manuscripts in the Bodleian Library and also some in the British Library in London – though I also hoped to see what I could of urban literacy in London, and, if possible, judge what implications it might have for my work in Washington.

I say "my work in Washington," and that too wants a footnote. For the past twenty-seven years I have directed a program in which Georgetown undergraduates travel twice a week to a low-rise apartment complex called "Sursum Corda," there to instruct K-5 children in the language arts. The name of the complex was taken from the Preface of the Latin mass, and means, "Lift up your hearts;" the response of the people is: "We have lifted them up to the Lord." The construction of Sursum Corda was organized by a group of Catholic laymen intent on providing housing for low and moderate income families that had been displaced by what was then called "Urban Renewal," which, whatever else it was, was also a convenient way of forcing the poor from their homes. It was built with help from the federal dollars (then-Senator Robert F. Kennedy of New York was instrumental in securing funding) between 1968 and 1970, one of five such apartment complexes then constructed in the area: the others involved church and civic groups, including the Baptists and the Masons. Sursum Corda is made up of 199 town houses that serve as residential units, with 5 reserved for other purposes (laundry, administrative offices, and a public library, since closed). It covers almost four-and-a-half acres, or somewhat more than five-and-a-half if streets and sidewalks are included, an important distinction just now, when the complex's demolition is being actively considered. When we began work it housed almost 1500 residents, but has fewer now.

The program was begun by a group of Catholic laymen who associated themselves with the Reverend Horace McKenna, S.J., a Jesuit priest originally involved with the poor and disadvantaged in a particularly racist part of southern Maryland. There his work had led to confrontation with the deeply racist KKK, so that his order had insisted that, for his own preservation, he move to Washington. The Jesuits staffed a parish church close to what became Sursum Corda, and he had settled in there, drawn to the soon to be displaced community, and then into the planning of the new one, Sursum Corda. When we began our program there he was still well remembered under what had become his "Sursum Corda name": Father Makenny. In fact in those days almost everyone at Sursum Corda had a "Sursum Corda name": a mother named Katherine who had a daughter of the same name became Big Cat and Little Cat, a boy became "Ears," another "Eyes," and a third "Dukie." But memories of the money he brought when the rent was due, and food when it was needed, preserved his name well after he had died. He had also begun our program, convincing some of his brother Jesuits at Georgetown to organize a bus to bring 10 or so students weekly to the new community at Sursum Corda to help children with their homework, and so it was in those happy days before drugs appeared in the community, and changed everything.

The program I became associated with in 1989, soon after the community was established, and was overflowing both with good intentions and with general ignorance about what the students could or should do. In the early days, the Georgetown students would travel to Sursum Corda in a school bus, or even, when the numbers became small enough, in a car, and then go on foot to the house where they knew their young learners awaited them, really to work on homework, which too often was far beyond the children, and which they failed to understand. But even that relatively simple agenda was in doubt: the houses in which they worked often held children of different ages and grade levels, so that the possibility of working with one in particular could not always be accomplished. Again, the parents sometimes regarded the program as free babysitting, and would leave shortly after the student arrived, so that when the hour was up, and the student had to leave, he or she often walked out of a house now without adult supervision. But even the walk back to the Community Center where the bus or car was parked could be contested, particularly for young women, who were sometimes the object of catcalls. The situation became such that parents who understood it would often direct their child to accompany the tutor back to the waiting bus, so that their reason for being in the community would be apparent, and the tutor would be spared the catcalls. It was not, in many respects, an entirely happy situation, and became a good deal less so when, in the early 1980's, drugs appeared, and very soon were everywhere.

In the fall of 1989, however, the university officials who, from a certain distance, oversaw the program came to understand that changes were indicated, and made them. The work of the program, the "tutoring," would henceforth take place inside an upstairs room in the Community Center, an administrative building that includes a large, cinder block room one floor up, that was readily adaptable to teaching. The university also hired a member from the community to work with the program, thus securing children who could be counted on to come regularly. It also sought advice from an experienced primary school teacher, the wife of a Georgetown philosophy professor, who had been successfully teaching 5 to 8 year-old children in Washington for some years, but whose strict commitment to phonics proved problematic, even though what she advised was certainly better than what had been in place before. She herself was warm, engaging and sophisticated, and her presence helped to establish the proposition that there were at last to be rules and direction, and that working with the language arts, not homework, was the new direction, and it was to be observed.

Although the age of the children varied over the years, we gradually moved toward working with young children, most often between the ages of 5 and 9, and primarily in the language arts – understood by us to include reading, writing, listening, speaking

-- but the first two most of all. Over the years virtually everything changed, and changed again: we began with teaching the children one-on-one once a week, but made much more effective progress when, some time later, we increased our weekly sessions to two; in round numbers, our program taught 50 learners, but gradually decreased to 25 when we increased the hours; and it changed again when I attached it to an English Department elective course, which enabled me to ask even more of the students who take part, a practice that continues to this day.

But after a year I understood that, in spite of the assistance we had received, I needed to know more than I did about what went into student instruction. I read university catalogues that described summer courses and programs in Education, and decided on the University of California at Berkeley. I then approached the Dean of the College for a grant to cover both Berkeley's tuition, suspiciously low for courses in education, and also money to live there, which he, knowing the object, allowed. A word from a colleague who had studied at Berkeley directed me to live in International House, universally known as I-House, a graduate dormitory that even in the summer provides accommodation for American and overseas students and for visiting scholars; it proved ideal for my purposes. There was, and I have no doubt still is, an open-mindedness present throughout I-House that was welcoming and attractive even by Berkeley standards, though many of the residents, including those from overseas, were rather more affluent than the Berkeley norm, and in general less interested in the world beyond their campus. But it was for me a happy choice. Years later I would seek, unsuccessfully, to interest the then I-House administration in establishing a program for its residents to work with urban children, many of them disadvantaged, in near-by Oakland, and although the then-Director embraced the proposed project warmly, its implementation was frustrated, if rumor can be believed, by those in his administration who estimated that doing so would only increase their responsibilities.

The courses that I took in the School of Education of the University of California at Berkeley provided an overview of current educational theories and practices that in due course contributed greatly to our program. It was while I was there I became interested in the brilliant Russian psychologist Lev Vygotsky (1896-1934) and his almost equally perceptive American advocate, Professor Jerome Brenner of New York University, who effectively made his work known in the West.

Lev Vygotsky was born in 1896, and spent his childhood in the Russian city of Gomel, the second of eight children of a middle-class Jewish bank manager who provided his son with a personal tutor until he reached the age to attend the public gymnasium. From the beginning he was a decided polymath, interested in philosophy, particularly Hegel, aesthetics and literature, particularly Shakespeare, and inscribing a long early essay on *Hamlet*. In spite of the prejudice he encountered, he enrolled in the medical school of Moscow University in 1913, but soon transferred to Law, graduating in 1917. He developed his increasingly well-known work in psychology and cognitive studies until his death, from tuberculosis, in 1934. By 1936 many of his newer methods and much of his later thinking had been rejected state authorities, though certain of his students were able to carry on some aspects of his work.

I encountered Vygotsky in the course of a visiting professor whose interest I came to share, and although what attracted me to him initially was his justly famous "zone of proximal development," I was taken as well by his constructivist understanding of learning, and by his focus on the role that social interaction played in the development of cognition. I was struck too by his insistence upon the activist role of the child, and by the way he had moved the study of education from an examination of knowledge acquisition and personal development to that of social mediation and interaction. Given the Georgetown program that then concerned me, I became increasingly interested in the nature of that interaction, and read eagerly Alex Kozulin's revised edition of Vygotsky's *Thought and Language* (1994), noting how Vygotsky spoke to certain limitations of the learning process once current, so perhaps pointing toward what I came to think of as an actual exchange between student and child, an exchange that spoke, if indirectly, both to the agency of the Georgetown student, and to the response, informed by sociocultural circumstances, of the Sursum Corda child, a response that very often engaged and so informed the older student. This dynamic invariably lead to certain forms of conventional instruction as well, but a sense of mutual interaction remained, and the exchange, often initiated and usually guided by the older student, informed the occasion.

Subsequently, I became interested in a rich collection of essays Kozulin later edited with others, *Vygotsky's Educational Theory in Cultural Context* (2003), that dealt, in an essay by Pedro Portes and Jennifer Vadeboncoeur, with the role of socioeconomic status in cognitive socialization, one of several that came to inform my understanding, and, to a degree at least, our practice. No doubt the literary convention that is now called interrogation, posing questions that are not strictly called for by the text, played a part in my apprehension, but the nature of the questions that Vygotsky posed and addressed played an undoubted role in the development of our program.

I was informed as well by a study that Ken and Yetta Goodman had contributed to Luis Moll's collection of essays, *Vygotsky and Education* (1990) that linked Vygotsky's thinking to their own foundational work in Whole Language. Among other things, Whole Language emphasizes that children work best when they experience a high degree of autonomy in their learning, the more so, Vygotsky might have said, if it is shared with an older learner, in a meaningful and authentic transaction. In some ways Vygotsky seemed to me to add an edge and even a direction to Whole Language, and in the context of the program that then engaged me, a welcome one indeed. Thus when, in due course, the Wadham program moved away from an in-class teacher's aide model to one more invested in mutual engagement, I welcomed the development as a particularly appropriate alteration. Sometimes, as when the Normans or the Aztecs were under examination, the class dynamic took the model of what I can only call a seminar, albeit one that mixed semi-Whole Language with semi-Vygotskian strategies.

This development was brought about, however, during the program's first decade, when the Reverend Doctor Harriet Harris was Wadham's Chaplain, working with the then-Head Teacher at Hermitage, Abdul-Hayee Murshad, a perceptive and able young administrator, in order to develop a working arrangement for students in the Wadham program. They did so, needless to say, without reference to the strategies I have described here, though they were ones indicated during the years the program had been advancing. Thus, although the connection between the combination of influences mentioned here and what we shall later observe in London should not be overstated, these strategies indicate the direction in which the program moved, in a way similar to the direction they supplied to my own work at Sursum Corda. Vygotsky's honest thought, like that of Ken and Yetta Goodman, pointed toward a common good that, changes having been made, was our objective too, if coincidentally.

    At Sursum Corda, in the early days, that thought had a more immediate effect as well. In the first place, it moved us away from what was for our students a somewhat uncritical reliance on phonics, and helped to introduce a variety of Whole Language teaching strategies that Georgetown students came somewhat to understand, and that encouraged them to engage their young learners thoughtfully but also imaginatively, and with a focus first and last upon comprehension. In fact as time went on, our program at Sursum Corda developed two mottos, not unconnected with these influences. The first, intended for the tutor's first four or five weeks, reasonably enjoined him or her: "Don't Prompt Too Quickly." The second, intended for all of the days following, read simply: "Comprehension, Comprehension, Comprehension." Particularly when we began, and when most of our students attended the same public (British English = state) school, one that was deeply invested in phonics, it was not at all uncommon for a child to be able to read accurately a page put before him or her, but be quite unable to say what the passage actually meant. We employed the usual ways of addressing this difficulty – previewing and prediction strategies -- and encouraging the tutors to seek out such high interest texts as encouraged comprehension, and to begin a conversation there. As time went on we deepened our expectation of the exchange between student and learner, encouraging the student to ensure comprehension less by asking factual questions, than by posing those requiring interpretation, often asking "Why," or requiring individual application (What would you have done?), or even by posing questions involving values (Was what the boy did right?). If we had patron saints in those early days, I would be inclined to name not only my creative if astringent Russian Lev Vygotsky, but also the brilliant New Zealand educator Marie Clay, whose focus on comprehension equally contributed to our project.

When we began there, however, Sursum Corda, like many communities in Washington in those days, was no stranger to the drug trade, and as a result there was about a murder a month in and around it, usually in the small hours. In the first year, however, there was a spectacular murder on a Saturday afternoon just before we began work, in which a ski-masked gunman with an uzi submachinegun shot his victim in the face, at close range, spilling the young man's brains onto the pavement in front of the Community Center where, on Tuesday and Thursday evenings, we continue to hold our lessons. The event was observed by some of the children in our program who happened to be there at the time, one of whom later wrote an essay concerning the event, alluding with horror to the "white worms," the brains, that had poured out of the young man's head.

Another actually took place during the course of a tutoring session, and when it was understood what had happened, the session was curtailed and everyone left quickly. But these were unusual. Often, as in the first case I described, the killer knew the victim, and became quickly known himself to the victim's family, with predictable results. Sometimes they were friends: one young man, on a contract, shot his friend in the chest rather than in his face, apparently in deference to their friendship. In another case the killer murdered the wrong sibling – but then returned two weeks later for the right one.

Because I acknowledge, of course, that my work at Sursum Corda contributed to the English programs that I helped to develop and advise, I should note some at least of the evident academic differences between them: while the Wadham program moved from one-on-one teaching, to classroom instruction, to what almost amount to seminars, the Georgetown program remained rooted in one-on-one tutoring. Thus as we began to understand what could be asked of the students who took part, we developed these practices: ascertaining, as far as we could, that the students should understand what was expected of them, and also what they actually might be able to accomplish, not in their wildest dreams, but in reality. In Washington, our focus was to support, but also to develop, our learners' comprehension in the language arts, with a particular emphasis on reading and writing. It became apparent too that my   expectation of this progress, though it varied according to child and tutor both, had to be realistic, expecting miracles only rarely, if at all. But progress there was, and it was not uncommon even in our first year for one of our young learners to experience a sudden im-provement, as he or she began to read with an unexpected fluency, and so make a breakthrough, or at least reach a new plateau.

In the early days of the Wadham program, as we shall see, we sought a close connection with Hermitage, however, with students working in classrooms as teachers' aides, though in due course it became apparent that the real value of the program, as I have already said, was encouraging young children to understand what a university was, and that it was an evident good, even to them, young as they were. The larger proposition was to suggest that attending one might prove, one day, an attractive proposition. What mattered was that, as we shall see, the Wadham, and later the Clare College students, would connect with the Tower Hamlets children over matters of at least apparently mutual interest, getting to know and trust each other, so that, once or twice a year, when the visit was returned, the children would feel a measure of familiarity by seeing the students again, albeit in a new setting. The "matters of mutual interest" came to include topics that the children had been set to study, Normans and Aztecs and others. These topics, to be sure, were often supported by exhibitions that were on offer in London museums (the British Museum exhibition on the Aztecs was particularly impressive), but they were also topics that university students could find out about in their college libraries without great disruption to their other studies. The result was that both groups of students could appear very well informed, and so able to engage each other in meaningful discourse.

The other advantage of the shift in direction was that it necessitated fewer visits to the schools from the Oxford and Cambridge colleges, though it invested those that did take place, once or twice a term as it turned out, with greater impact and meaning, and emphasized that these new teacher-colleagues had come from a university: a word known by all, but understood only imperfectly. The movement from teacher's aide to colleague-teacher was in keeping not only with the time in which university students might pursue an evident social objective usually unconnected to their own academic responsibilities, but it also engaged them in understanding, in some cases perhaps more deeply than they had done, something at least of the evident social differences present in Britain today. Certain of these, students would sometimes say, seem to be underrepresented in current cultural discourse, except when an apparently related issue, like the role of Muslim influence in Birmingham state schools, presented itself. An understanding of such larger concerns, though not integral to the Wadham or the Clare College programs, became in time implicit, and a part of the experience of the students who were involved in them, so that learning could easily become a two-way street, and interests were awakened that could persist.

2

Another Oxford

Pembroke College and Hermitage School—Inter-Ethnic Rivalry—Washington and London Again—Attachments in Tower Hamlets—Gower Street and Brick Lane—Ethnic Minorities, State Schools

In 1992 I was, somewhat to my surprise but very much to my delight, elected to a visiting fellowship at Pembroke College, Oxford, where I had previously been a student. My project was to examine a number of English medieval manuscripts, primarily of the fourteenth and fifteenth century, that were directly relevant to studies I had been conducting on late medieval English poetry and some forms of religious belief. I had been alerted to the opportunity, which had been advertised in the *Oxford Gazette*, by Professor Douglas Gray, a former teacher at Pembroke, who had for many years been a fellow in medieval literature there for many years, before being elected the first J. R. R. Tolkien Professor in the university, and my application was further supported by the great Samuel Johnson bibliographer David Fleeman, then Senior English Fellow at Pembroke. It proved to be a fruitful appointment, which allowed me both to return to manuscripts I had not seen for some years, and to examine new ones. It was thus of real help in work that I am still carrying on.

By then I had been working at Sursum Corda for three years, and was interested to learn what I could about urban literacy in London, in particular in state schools, whose American equivalents had, in those days in Washington, an unenviable reputation. Before setting out on my search, however, I thought it right to let authorities in Pembroke know what I was about, so described the venture both to David Fleeman, who encouraged it warmly, and to the internationally famous four-minute-miler and then-Master of Pembroke Sir Roger Bannister, who in a perfectly friendly way pointed out that it contradicted no requirement of my fellowship, so there could be no objection to it. David in particular could be a stickler, but it was with him I concluded that my interests were perfectly consonant, since a six year-old child is every bit as complicated as a medieval manuscript, though a good deal more precious. Thus it was that after settling in at Pembroke I made my way to the Institute of Education in London in order to inquire how I might pursue this second objective.

This proved to be a lesson in itself. The woman at the information desk kindly directed me to a particularly perceptive member of the Institute, who proved sympathetic if a little dubious about my undertaking, but first of all suggested that I sit in on some of the lectures there, so that I could understand better how the Institute functioned, and also, I divined, so that they could take a somewhat closer look at me. I agreed at once though doing so necessitated weekly trips to London, which became possible only when two most generous friends, Charlotte and Mossman Roueché, learned Byzantinists both, generously offered weekly overnight accommodation, a *sine qua non* that happily included advice as well, and extended into subsequent months. Years later, Charlotte, who had followed the project and advised me over the years, would suggest that I write this book. But it was through their hospitality that, in due course, I was able to return first to the Institute, then to a particular school early on Tuesday morning, since I could stay with them on Monday night.

After a few weeks at the Institute I had evidently passed muster, and was asked if I would like to visit a number of different schools in the less affluent reaches of London, visits that the Institute could arrange. But by then I had decided that I was in no position to interrogate such places effectively (or at all), and asked instead if I might work one day a week in a school that served disadvantaged, or at least culturally diverse children, perhaps offering reading support in exchange, based on my work at Berkeley, to such children as required it.

For reasons I never fully understood (the Head Teacher was not well known in the Institute), the school selected for me was Hermitage Primary School in Vaughan Way, Wapping, a short walk from Tower Hill tube stop, and, as it turned out, ideal for my purposes and instruction. A week later I appeared there, somewhat apprehensively if truth be told, described (what was already known) my Institute of Education connection and introduced myself. I was warmly received first by the smart and perceptive Head Teacher, and then given a most friendly welcome by the staff, and encouraged to work with four children in particular, who indeed needed such practice and support as I could supply. I worked in the year two classroom, whose excellent homeroom teacher had, coincidentally, returned from Berkeley only a year or two earlier, where her scientist husband had been studying. On the first day we discussed the advantages and limitations of that excellent little city, including its useful public library, rich in children's books, and its affordable ethnic restaurants. She was thoughtful, insightful and dedicated to her children. I could hardly have had a better leader.

Before its expansion, Hermitage School was an intimate but lively institution, whose well-lit and open classrooms gave onto a central schoolyard through one door, and into the school itself through another. Teachers met easily and often, and in general the tone was supportive but focused, so that the multiethnic, if largely Bangladeshi student body knew itself to be well looked after, encouraged but not indulged, with attention paid to its diversity, but not only to that.

The first day was the liveliest, with two children holding hands and looking up at me in the schoolyard, very clearly talking to each other about me, secure in the knowledge that I could not understand a word that they were saying. And in the middle of a reading lesson a girl approached me in tears, devastated by the circumstance that another child's family had somehow acquired her family's "fimla," and she would never see it again. "O Lord," I thought, what is this all about? But then I had a quite unexpected brainwave, and realized that a "fimla" was very likely nothing more than a video cassette, a "film," which had simply been borrowed by the family of a friend, and would no doubt someday be returned. Tears stopped, peace was restored. For whatever reason the children took to me as I to them, so that, a few weeks later, when one of them asked me why I only came on Tuesday, and I foolishly used the word "library" in my explanation, he at once insisted that that was no reason at all, and I should instead use the perfectly good one that was in his school.

Over the course of my time there I had good luck with three of the four children to whom I had been assigned, but less so with the fourth, who lived with his grandfather, and resisted instruction from women teachers, but not from me who was male. His grandfather's attitudes may have informed him in other ways too: on a field trip to the Natural History Museum in Kensington, he responded to the kind ministrations of a tall black man who was directing the children where to hang up their coats by smiling up at him and saying what sounded like, "Kali bandor." The teacher who was with us, one of the few white teachers in the school to speak Sylheti, the Bengali dialect favored in Wapping, waited until the man had left, and then remonstrated with the boy, black himself, for what he had said. Apparently, and in spite of his smile, what he had replied was, "Black monkey." Later I described the incident to the Head Teacher, by then a friend, and added how disheartening inter-ethnic rivalry could be, particularly when seen among the young. But she considered that where power and exploitation do not exist, such rivalry invariably rested upon other circumstances – naiveté, for example, or lack of education, or imitation based on ignorance, and that it could be addressed and treated.

Subsequently, I tried to suspend judgment on such encounters, and to remember how misleading preconceptions can be. But as the years went on I was struck how different many of the circumstances I encountered in Washington were from those I found in London. In Washington, among disadvantaged and usually black families, it was not unusual to find parents who fought shy of the educational establishment as a whole, which in context often meant avoiding the local primary school that their children attended. We would sometimes discuss this issue in the community with whose leaders we consulted, and would have it pointed out to us that the scars inflicted in primary school can be long-lasting, so that if parents themselves had a hard passage there, or if they simply couldn't read, they might be disinclined to engage the school in any meaningful way, still less to attend a "Parent's Night." And indeed towards the end of our first semester working at Sursum Corda, one of our young tutors was explaining to the parents of the boy he had been teaching about the reading progress their son had made, only to be told that they were not concerned with that. He would always have television for entertainment, they insisted, and what was important was that he learn arithmetic, so that he would not be cheated when he spent money. Later, a helpful member of the community suggested that a good reply might have been to agree about the importance of arithmetic, but to point out too how useful reading would be in the future, particularly when their son had to sign a contract.

Communications with the local community in Tower Hamlets exist as well, both in the inclusion of community members among the school's Governors, and also, in the past at least, as members from the community, fluent in the local dialect and in English, who were engaged to assist the schools in various ways – in speaking to the children in their own dialect, for example, or more memorably, in translating between parents and teachers or parents and administrators, when necessary. These appointments have been curtailed, but they reminded me of like circumstances that obtained at a Catholic primary school in Washington in the early 1990's, when a large number of undocumented Spanish-speaking children sought to enroll, who, in the early days, were sometimes introduced to the organization and operation of their classrooms by their fellow students, who alone were bilingual. The situation was soon remedied, Spanish being widely available in Washington, and the situation in public (state) schools was aided as well by a 1974 Supreme Court decision, Lau v. Nichols, directing that schoolchildren not be refused admission to any public school for their inability to speak English. The Judgment further required that the children's inability to speak English had to be taken into account in their subsequent instruction. It was an excellent judgment, but as such was of course not funded (that would be left to the states), and so was hardly implemented overnight.

I understand that all comparisons, especially those connected to as delicate a topic as this one, can be invidious, and that any generalization is subject to revision. But early on in my introduction to Tower Hamlets, both from what I saw among the children with whom I worked, and from what I was able to observe in the general population of the school, I was struck by evident differences with what I had seen in Washington. No doubt differences in the focus and direction of the teaching can account for some of it, but in London there seemed to me an element of familiarity and of hope for what might develop in time to come, even without any concerted attempt to address cultural difference. In each case the requirements and expectations of the school differ from those of the community, but they are in dialogue with them too, consciously or not, according to the understanding of the Head Teacher or the Principal. But differences there were, and in Washington directions in the assignment of homework (not usually assigned in British state schools at so early an age) could issue from a central, downtown office, in a way that would have been unthinkable in London. The difficulty with the American practice is that when orders are sent without a clear understanding of the specific circumstances they are intended to address, they can be most unhelpful indeed. In the end, it is hardly possible in many cases to say who is most "at fault," a school that cannot meet expectations or the administrators who formulate those expectations. But often, in America at least, the choice usually falls upon the school.

But in some cases parents seemed to understand the end toward which we were seeking to lead their children, so that their interest was kindled by the possibilities being held out. Similar attitudes exist among disadvantaged families everywhere, and there are many American programs, some state, some federal, many private, that encourage aspiration. What such projects turn on is often the realization that many smart, intellectually lively children, and particularly those from disadvantaged families, simply do not achieve the intellectual potential of which they give clear evidence in childhood, but which could be developed in higher education, could they but reach it.

But how? The focus of this book falls upon one Oxford and one Cambridge program, but during this time I advised another program as well, staffed by University of London students from the Catholic Chaplaincy in Gower Street, who directed their work largely to Christ Church School, a Church of England school in Brick Lane, largely composed of Bangladeshi children. Before beginning there I discussed the program with the Head Teacher, who sadly (for us: in fact it was a promotion) was about to leave the school after more than twenty years there, but welcomed us anyway, since she knew about the Hermitage program, and was interested in it. I began to explain what we do, and she interrupted to say, in effect, Yes, that's fine. Do what you want. What I want is for the children to meet university students, and really to know who they are, and that it's no bad thing to leave London. Most of these children don't want to leave Tower Hamlets, never mind London. One of my greatest disappointments after 20 years here is to see very, very bright children refuse to apply to university, or if at all, only to the local polys. They are at least as bright as my son (who, we had already established, was graduating from Peterhouse, Cambridge, in a month's time), but though I know they are wrong, many don't think they will be welcome outside London.

Now it is a decade later, and I am discussing with Zoe Howe the thoughtful and insightful Head Teacher at Hermitage the same issue, one she has talked about with her fellow Heads, almost all of whom share her concern. But she has taken a novel approach, and has obtained a bursary from Lloyd's Bank – Viva Lloyd's Bank! – for 350 pounds, to take a class for a day trip to a beach in France, with a mission there to buy an ice cream cone and also (I assume) have a swim. There was, of course, much that needed to be done in order to accomplish these good objectives, but it turned into a real success, one that was embraced both by the children and by their families, and that has now been several times repeated. Not long after one of these trips we were holding a meeting in one of the schools for a small group of Head Teachers and others who were concerned with this and with other matters relevant to our programs, and to this meeting we had invited two Camden representatives, who were smart, helpful in their comments, and seemed to be quite interested in the discussion. But when we renewed the discussion and repeated the invitation a few months later they sent quite a junior colleague in their place, a young white man, who seemed to resent the topic. As we began, and as I was reopening the discussion in the light of the recent trip to France, he interrupted, and would have none of it. Why, he demanded, should Bangladeshi students have any concern at all for their reception anywhere in Britain? Any such concern is as childish as it was for his little girls changing schools, who were apprehensive before they went, but were reassured, and it all went perfectly well. It's no different from that. His position in Camden is somehow concerned with Bangladeshi families in Tower Hamlets, and he felt strongly that if there had been a problem he would have known about it. Really, there was nothing for them to worry about at all, he assured us, and (what he only implied) he did not like to hear the issue mooted, especially, I thought, by me.

But the issue is a real one, whether in Britain or America, and without a certain effort it can be difficult for the young to cross what certainly can appear to be unfriendly borders. Some years ago an affluent Jesuit high school in Washington became concerned that it had enrolled relatively few Latino students, and, having secured some scholarship money (tuition there was $7,000 a year), approached the Principal (Head Teacher) of a near-by Catholic elementary and middle school that enrolled very many in order to secure her best student. The woman in charge of the school was Cuban, and a good deal more knowledgeable than the well-meaning Jesuits about the challenges her children would be likely to face. Of course she would be delighted to work with them, she insisted, and she was not unaware of the advantages they were holding out to her children. But surely they could understand that she could not send only one student, especially to a school that had so few Latino students. Four was a better number, she thought. It was a better beginning, and could lead to greater things. And it would not isolate anyone.

No doubt these analogies are far from exact, and probably the differences are what should be remembered. But there are incentives not to apply for anything among those who are not members of the prevailing culture, which in America means white and middle class. True enough, in these days at least, an Einstein or an Emerson or a Wordsworth would stand a better chance of being spotted than in years past, but what of one not, or not yet, quite so good? The first day students from Clare visited the children at Bigland Green Primary School, there was a certain excitement in the air, mixed with apprehension on both sides. True enough, the children in years 5 and 6 knew what a university was. They even knew, somewhat at least, what it meant to attend Cambridge. But even so, there was much for them to learn.

A friend tells me that Parliament – though to my American ear he seems to mean the Department of Education -- is largely unworried about students who don't apply to Oxford. Their interest, he says, is in those from state schools who do apply, and are turned down. But as for bright and able students who don't apply for reasons of race, status or culture -- so be it. Still, when all is said and done, the incentive to challenge must finally come from within. Are the powers of the state really hostile to encouraging the very young, for fear that doing so will distract attention from those in year 12? The only good university is the one you're happy at. With quantity, consider difference too.

3

Beginning Work

Wadham's New Project—Reverend Doctor Giles Fraser—the Chaplaincy—Disadvantaged Children and Ethnic Minorities—An Example?—the Possible

Even though some aspects of academic life are quite opaque, it is generally understood that, at seven-year or seven-term intervals (though particularly in America the frequencies are changing), some universities offer the possibility of what in Britain is called study leave, in America sabbaticals, to faculty members. It is less widely understood that these leaves require a certain effort to acquire and to complete, and should not be confused with vacations, which, whether on leave or in the summer, many academics indulge too rarely. In 1999 I again received a sabbatical from Georgetown, one that I again sought to dedicate to the examination of certain medieval manuscripts in Oxford, London and Cambridge, in connection with some work on medieval lyrical poetry. Again I set out to find lodgings in Oxford, in the hope of remaining there for the course of one American semester, or two Oxford terms. There were certain visiting fellowships in Oxford for which I might apply, and happily I was awarded one of them, the Keeley Visiting Fellowship at Wadham College, named for one Thomas Keeley, a former fellow in physics who had in his will established it, and whose long residence in the college included secret missions to Germany before the War in order to discover where German science was in certain vital areas. My mission was less hazardous, and the award included membership in Wadham's Senior Common Room, most dinners, and implicit permission to rent a flat in a university house on Bradmore Road, in North Oxford. By mid January 2000 I had done so, settled in, and begun work in Bodley, as the excellent university library is informally and affectionately known.

The Senior Common Room consisted in a large, conveniently situated, sitting room, provided with coffee, newspapers, magazines and sherry, and membership there made it relatively easy to meet the college fellowship, old and young. It was presided over formally by a warm and perceptive scientist, who both liked the fellowship and was liked in return, and who was informally supported too by his wife, a lively Francophile who counted the wife of the Warden (as the Head of Wadham is called), among her friends, and who thus made a useful and happy bridge between the Warden, his wife and the fellowship, since, to the surprise of this American, in Wadham as in other Oxford colleges, the Head of House is not a member of the Senior Common Room *ex officio*, and so appears there only rarely, and usually by invitation.

Neither is the college chaplain a member, but Wadham's chaplain in those days was the Reverend Doctor Giles Fraser, whose time (and salary) were divided between Wadham and St. Mary's, the university church on High Street, a circumstance that the college bore as best it could. In subsequent years he became well know in Britain, whether through his thoughtful and witty work in the Guardian newspaper or through his many television appearances. More recently still he has become even better known in Britain thanks to his impressive and principled stand, as Dean of St. Paul's cathedral in London, for his support of the "Occupy Wall Street" movement when it arrived at St. Paul's, and that sadly led to his resignation on what was clearly a matter of principle. When we met, however, he was a widely esteemed, smart and lively college chaplain, familiar to students in other colleges who sometimes came to his services, and known for the ways in which he engaged students intellectually, whether through movies or through philosophy — his D.Phil. thesis had been on Kierkegaard — and in due course we became friends.

At some point not long after returning to Oxford I revisited Hermitage School, both to renew friendships and also to see what interest there might be in having any Wadham students who were interested come to the school and work informally with the children there. There are, of course, closer schools to Oxford than this one, but Tower Hamlets is a place unto itself, and I estimated that the cultural encounters between children and students might prove mutually and agreeably beneficial, and develop an interest the university among children for whom it was but a word.

Cultural interaction in a school is of a different character than it is elsewhere, the more so when it is reinforced by differences in age and, sometimes at least, in social and economic status. The school sets appropriate limits on the nature and degree of the interaction, but not ones that are onerous, and, as we subsequently discovered, irregular interventions have an effect all their own. The important thing is that there should be an exchange, with each side intending to learn about the other, content to consider whatever the topic under discussion may be, and at least somewhat curious about the interaction itself. In London as in Washington, a sense that the child or the student is in some way "other" can stimulate the interchange, at least initially, though as the interaction deepens, as it can do rather quickly, more personal qualities invariably emerge, and can precipitate the exchange further. It is not so much that children and students learn certain "things," though that takes place, as that they unlearn attitudes and assumptions that they have, all unwittingly, taken for granted, and put other, often better ones, in their place.

In Washington, students bring a variety of expectations to their first visit to the community that is called Sursum Corda – thinking the buildings much worse (or more often, much better) than what they had expected, the place itself smaller (or larger), and the children they are to teach, happy, friendly, lively, and smart – a circumstance that too often they had simply not anticipated. In London I remember being surprised that, as far as I could tell, the English students registered less expectation of cultural difference than their American counterparts, whether because they simply assumed it, or because their economic status was less differentiated, or because, as I preferred to believe, in London there were, for a complex of reasons, fewer media-forged manacles than there are in Washington. Among the young at least, what matters most in any real exchange is what is assumed before a word is said. But that is what any true dialogue would address.

In any case, once approached, and for reasons that I hope will become clear in the course of this narrative, the school was very willing to encourage such a program as we proposed, thanks in part to a visit they had had at some point from an Eton student, who had come regularly for some weeks and worked ably and well with the children, making more or less everyone understand how such an arrangement might work, while encouraging the consideration that university students might, by their presence, contribute to the operation of the classroom, and point the way towards a wider world. Still, many of the Wadham students had not been in Tower Hamlets before, and for some it was their first encounter with a powerful and effective Muslim community. But as it turned out, these considerations were not the only ones that mattered, since it was about then, when we were first discussing and organizing the program, a larger issue appeared both in and outside of the university.

A bright sixth-form woman from a state school in the north of England had very recently applied to Oxford's Magdalen College (there is one in Cambridge too, spelled Magdalene, to which we will return) for admission to its pre-medical program, and had been refused entry (the pre-med program at Magdalen is a very small one, tiny by American standards). The student's Head Teacher (or Principal), himself an American, had advised her to apply to Harvard, perhaps the best known American university in Britain, which had accepted her. Worse (from what was said to have been Oxford's point of view) was to come: her case became widely known, was discussed in the press and in parliament, and Gordon Brown, M.P., the most powerful Labour minister excepting only the Prime Minister himself, weighed in heavily, arguing that this was further evidence, if any was needed, of Oxford's well-known anti-state school bias, of its disdain for state school students generally, and of its inability and unwillingness to change its ways. I do not mean to overstate how far this incident assisted in founding our program, the more so since I myself dissent from Mr. Brown's loud judgment, but it did us no harm at all, even though a colleague who seemed to be knowledgeable about such things insisted that if the medical don at Magdalen would stop appearing on the BBC quite so often, things might yet calm down. But as Chaucer has it, the greatest clerks be not the wisest men.

Wadham College was founded in 1610 by Dorothy Wadham, then aged 75, who completed construction in only four years, directing everything from her home in Devon, and according to the terms of her late husband's will. She never saw the place. It was famed in its early years for offering a home to a scientific circle that developed into the Royal Society, and for numbering the great Sir Christopher Wren among its fellows. It is today widely believed to be one of the more progressive colleges in the university, but it also seemed to me one of the more humane, a circumstance that then depended upon the interaction of the Warden, John Flemming, with the fellowship, and with the Head of the Senior Common Room. Its tone also depended upon the relationship between students and fellows, which seemed to me formally informal, even when, as sometimes happens, students had to be called to account. Recent Wardens, including John Flemming, were known for having been particularly attentive to their students, and an earlier one, Sir Claus Moser, was still remembered for the student lunches and the musical evenings he had organized for undergraduates. One other example struck me at the time. Wadham enjoyed the good services of a particularly able senior fellow who taught medicine, and who was aware that his profession dealt with issues that could be difficult, even charged, for certain of his Catholic students. Among such he, an observant Anglican (and one with a fine ear for college choirs), seemed to me particularly thoughtful and perceptive, and his evident sympathy was understood not only by his students, but also in the Catholic Chaplaincy (many individual colleges maintain an Anglican chaplain, but there is only one Catholic chaplain for the university as a whole), where his sensitivity was understood and appreciated. Changes having been made, it seemed to me that his example could be multiplied many times. Wadham was then, and no doubt still is, an excellent place to be a student.

This combination of what seemed to me an institutional belief in its students (who had been chosen by the fellows themselves, not as in America, by an entirely separate "Office of Admissions"), and by a related willingness to let them chance their arm, seemed to me particularly helpful in getting the program up and running. Both Giles and I would discuss what was intended with whoever wished it, Giles no doubt more effectively than me, but the fellowship in general was confident of its students' ability to manage their own responsibilities. The Law Dons in particular were also sensitive to its advantages, both academic and institutional, perhaps because they were acutely aware of the new interest in college admissions from state schools that was taking place in parliament and in the press. No doubt Wadham's generally progressive attitudes did us some good too, but it seemed to me that we were helped as well by what I can only the tone of the college, what students of cinema call the *mis-en-scene*, and that, together with the interaction of the Warden, the Head of the SCR, a particularly able Chaplain, and certain supportive fellows, helped to bring it about, and sustained it for what became fifteen years.

Although I have emphasized the central role Giles Fraser played in the origin of the program, there is one other factor that is relevant. Giles was an impressive but not unusual combination of a high church Anglican priest who held quite progressive social attitudes, a combination that endeared him to many students, and to me. During the years I worked with him I was struck repeatedly by the humane and progressive attitudes high church Anglicans in particular often revealed when they spoke of the marginalized and the disadvantaged, and in most cases they seemed to me to have moved well beyond a sense of alms-giving to one of genuine respect, that often led to a felt concern for social equality. True enough, there are good persons everywhere who do not share this interest, indeed who reject it outright. A few years ago an American fundamentalist group let it be known that while they wished well to those whose religious practices involved not only the worship of God but also an investment in their neighbor, their religiousness embraced exclusively the former, from which all else was a distraction. Their belief was deeply felt, and, changes having been made, no doubt shared by other religious persons for whom such social engagement was not indicated.

Although at the time our program began the chaplaincy seemed to be the only place for it, in the intervening years many colleges have developed an "Outreach Office," that generally reports to whomever is directing the college, and that can absorb and channel whatever energy and money are dedicated to such activities. The relationship between this newish office and that of the chaplain is potentially important, though in certain places it is still being hammered out. Outreach offices can secure (sometimes by payment for services) the allegiance of students for specific programs, but in general their brief seems to be to help secure applications, in the hope that some admissions may follow, not to address undergraduates in such a way as to engage and move them. Rather they take up groups of students from outside the college, and do so with a clear purpose, one that can benefit the college and the potential applicant both.

No doubt there are priests in many denominations who, like some American fundamentalists, believe that issues of social justice are optional, and deserve no special place in their agenda. But particularly among the young, it has been my experience both in Washington and in London that the practice of social justice in a religious context can prove intrinsically valuable, and enlarge attitudes toward others, particularly when cultural or ethnic differences are present. The religion of the young is happiest in accomplishment and outcome, and however great or little that may be, its practice can involve personal change as well. Significant differences between Anglican and Catholic teachings concerning social justice, and those of other faiths as well, seem almost negligible to me, at least as far as practice is concerned. And that is one reason it may not be unreasonable to ask priests of whatever faith, perhaps in association with such secular colleagues as they esteem, to consider the advantages of such work – as many do.

Yet when the program began, Wadham was at least as well known for its atheists as for its Christians – though not among its chaplains, to be sure. The atheists, however, were a humane and friendly lot, and far from opposed to our project. One afternoon over lunch one group of them offered, facetiously to be sure, to found a supportive "Atheists for the Tower Hamlets Project." "To help supply money?" Giles gently inquired. Money is of course required for such work in order pay for student train and tube fares, but was generously supplied when Wadham's very knowledgeable director of development put a description of our program into a summer newsletter that was sent to alumni. It elicited well over a thousand pounds (if I ever knew the exact figure I have forgotten it), including what were said to be two checks for five hundred pounds each.

Since those brave beginnings both Oxford and Cambridge have expanded their outreach programs, dramatically shifting from university programs to ones attached to colleges. These have in the past sometimes involved bussing schoolchildren in to the colleges so that they can visit them, with the commendable intention of making them more familiar. These expeditions differ from, "Open Days," newly offered to students seeking entry under general admissions, and usually intended to encourage applications from good students applying in the usual way, with a sense of "Come to us, not to that grotty college across the street." Universities can of course seem forbidding, particularly to minority children, or to those whose parents never attended one. And indeed, some of the children who come on the trips can be so old (aged 17 or so from years 11 and 12) that it is difficult to believe that very many will be induced to apply as a result of such a late intervention.

Still, where college applications are concerned, attention to the individual student is probably what matters most of all. No doubt other practices by which colleges have sought to attract minority applications have been as effective too, and among Oxford colleges, as I have already mentioned, Pembroke in particular has distinguished itself, thanks in no small part to its outreach fellow and those who support him, for having focused on individual schoolchildren, many of them outside of Oxford, in subjects like classics and English, over a number of years. Summer programs too, particularly those supported by the Sutton Trust which have introduced future applicants both to the academic work and to the experience of living in Oxford, have rightly elicited much praise. In Cambridge, though there are other colleges in which the chaplaincies are involved in outreach, Clare College, which will figure prominently in this narrative, can perhaps claim a certain precedence, both for an exercise that I will describe in the next chapter, and also because of the high number of state school students whom it regularly admits. Like Wadham, Clare not only has a reputation for progressive practices, but as its website discloses, it too was effectively founded by a woman, Elizabeth de Burgh, Lady of Clare, who in 1359 made possible a charter to a university hall that began life in 1326, making it the second oldest college in Cambridge, after Peterhouse. Its seventeenth-century buildings are somewhat grander than Wadham's, but it seems to me to share Wadham's felt concern for the welfare of its students.

In the furtherance of outreach programs, however, the kingdom of Great Britain, and the City of London, have been divided up among Oxford and Cambridge colleges so that each college has been assigned certain areas of the country and certain parts of London, in which to recruit and generally to encourage student applications. The areas are repeated, however, so that Tower Hamlets is assigned, for outreach purposes, both to Wadham College, Oxford, and to Clare College, Cambridge. In general, and apart from programs like Pembroke's, few relationships between college and city can really be described as intimate, and it is only when a college, while not omitting its putatively larger outreach commitments, develops a relationship with one or more schools that it can hope to contribute effectively to the education of individual children, and do so by introducing them to an understanding of the university. What the Wadham program sought to do was to begin, and then to advance, a process of inquiry, and to do so among children who were, effectively if not formally, separated by social and sometimes by economic circumstances from understanding what a university is, and what its use to them might be. In time, the role of the Wadham students advanced from that of co-teacher to that of co-learner, as they engaged in conversation about matters of apparently mutual interest – Normans and Aztecs again – and began to engage each other intimately. The school to which the Wadham students came welcomed them not only for the proto-seminar they brought with them, but also for the larger attitudes of which they gave evidence, ones that spoke, however indirectly, to race and class as well as to Normans and Aztecs, and that brought voices that, while unfamiliar, were friendly and welcoming and engaged. But the boundaries to be crossed were real ones, and involved differences of age, of place, of race, of attitude, and of disposition.

4

Apogee

Taking Root—Reverend Doctor Harriet Harris—the Program(me) Develops—Hermitage Visits Oxford—Clare College, Cambridge—Reverend Doctor Gregory Seach—Whitechapel and Wapping—Mr. Abdul-Hayee Murshad and Ms. Zoe Howe—Stepeney Green—An Experiment at Clare

I

There is one person without whom the Wadham program would not have come about: the Reverend Doctor Harriet Harris, now the Chaplain at the University of Edinburgh, but for the nine years following Giles' departure, its effective and excellent director. Like most able chaplains, Giles did not regard his time at Wadham as intended to last forever, though it was evident that he enjoyed his work there, and it was on his watch that the program was formally announced, on May Day 2000, at a somewhat sparsely attended Evensong where I delivered the homily. The service was followed by some bottles of white wine in the fellows' garden, during which the choir informally sang Mozart cantatas and conversation was general. But when, not long after that, the parish of Putney in London, the one where the 1647 debates had taken place, sought a new pastor, Giles applied, largely, he intimated, because he found in Putney that mixture of High Church reflection and concern for the disadvantaged that had always engaged him. In that our project followed him. Coming from Oxford, our sympathies were also with those who sought a level playing field, and we were willing to dig to make it so. Thus in the end we were levelers one and all, and our debates were on exclusion too. The end-of-year party at which the college took leave of Giles and others was at once joyous and painful – the organ scholar was leaving as well and had to be thanked, and there were enough presents going around to cause the amused Warden to remark on what seemed to him a kind of ritual exchange of gifts worthy of anthropological examination.

Changes came with Harriet in the fall, and were all to the good. Harriet at once understood how the program sought to introduce children to an understanding of what the university is, and stands for, by letting them meet with university students both formally and informally, and saw too what Giles and I had missed, the necessity of inviting the children back to Oxford, so that they could begin to understand something of the university itself. In the years following, this "return visit" came to mean so much to those concerned with their students' reluctance to venture outside of London, that it became central to the operation. It all began with Harriet.

It is quite impossible to enumerate all of the changes Harriet introduced during the nine years she directed the program, over a period when I was usually back in Georgetown, but I have indicated that this was our apogee, because it was toward the end of the first decade that the program best flourished, and that, as we shall see shortly, it first appeared elsewhere. Throughout this time it was directed by Harriet, who was particularly good at discussing things with the students who took part, and incorporating their ideas when she discussed with Abdul-Hayee Murshad, the new Head Teacher, how they could best move forward. It was interesting to notice, over time, how many of the students were themselves members of groups not always first associated with the university, women, Muslims, French and American students. As a general rule such students, and whether in Georgetown or in Oxford, take their work most seriously, and understand, better than others, its possible effect. But in those early years it was Harriet who understood better than anyone what could be accomplished and what couldn't, and it was through her that the program came to take the shape it did, addressing topics that the children were considering in class, and not only at Hermitage, but sometimes in a hastily arranged seminar when they came to Wadham too, and also organizing the instructional and fun trips they took around Oxford when they visited.

Most of these trips engaged and amused everyone involved in them: at one point, we took a group of Year 5's to the Great Hall at Christ Church, having been allowed entry to the college by a porter who, confronted with a group of students much younger than those with whom he usually had to contend, most kindly overlooked our failure to make a reservation. We had acted in the expectation that the association of the Great Hall with Harry Potter might engage them, but there were no clouds beneath the ceiling nor candles floating among them, and faces fell. Was this really the place? But if so where then were the clouds? The next day, however, all was restored. Year 5 returned to tell year 2 about their expedition, and nothing was lost in the telling. They were exactly the same. (Latterly I am told that the Hall at Hogwarts was a set.) Another visit from Hermitage found us to Bodley's Divinity School, the locus of the Hogwarts infirmary in another of the Harry Potter movies, and therein one shy young boy was delighted to find himself standing exactly on the spot that Harry Potter's bed had occupied in the movie.

A more regular venture took us to the Pitt-Rivers Museum, just inside the Natural History Museum. No doubt there are some shrunken heads within it somewhere, though we regularly missed them, but what found favor instead were the enormous skeletons of dinosaurs that all but fill the first room of the Natural History Museum. But my own favorite was our visit to the Ashmolean Museum, when for some reason (probably time) we couldn't get to the Pitt Rivers. Though largely Bangladeshi in those years, Hermitage usually had a number of other children too, many from families visiting London. That year there was among their number a young Chinese boy who spoke English fluently. I do not know now what gallery we were in, but at one point we confronted, among other things, Chinese inscriptions, one of which, with small smile, the boy read, in English, to his classmates. His classmates applauded.

Connecting with Harriet about all of this, she reminds me how the college responded to the program and the children. The Wadham students were most welcoming, and the fact that the children remembered faces from when the students had visited their school dispelled any sense of strangeness, so the children felt welcome from the start. Thanks to an indulgent garden staff, the children were allowed to play ball games and to run about in the fellows' garden, and (what may not have been strictly approved) to climb into the lap of the seated Maurice Bowra metal statue, itself in the form of a chair, where the Wadham students would photograph them. In the end, the children would often declare the expedition to Wadham was the best school trip ever. They developed a sense, as Harriet observed, that Wadham was theirs, a place outside Tower Hamlets in which they were very welcome. Younger children at Hermitage, having heard many a yarn, would look forward to their visit.

But it was simply true that, in Oxford, the children were made welcome by everyone they met. The staff in the hall was particularly welcoming and friendly, and it became a tradition that the children would have a lunch of fish and chips, followed by jelly and ice-cream, served up in Wadham's Hall (not its canteen), where the seventeenth-century hammered beam roof reminded everyone of Hogwarts. After lunch, in small groups, the children were allowed to visit some of the students' rooms – Harriet reminds me that we scrupulously followed the relevant guidelines and regulations concerning such visits – which fascinated the children particularly. One time only there was a minor hic-cup. A new Dean, unacquainted with the tradition of the visit, was suitably astonished to discover a group of lively school children, fresh from their long bus ride, rushing about the fellows' garden. He advanced to restore order, but, alerted by Harriet, quickly grasped what was happening, and perceptive man that he was, understood at once that there are sometimes things more important than order and decorum.

Thus it was that, during Harriet's years at Wadham, the program throve. During that time, four or more Wadham students would visit Hermitage School once or twice a term, and then twice a year, in the fall and in the spring, their visits would be returned by Hermitage children coming to Wadham. Still, the initial encounter with Oxford could prove a little problematic. One wet October day the children arrived at Wadham in the middle of a rainstorm, which precluded the energy-expending game in the garden, so necessary after a long ride. As a result, we marched into Wadham's somewhat austere seventeenth-century chapel, made attractive by its stained glass, for what proved to be, for many of the children, their first encounter with a Christian house of worship. There the new Warden had kindly agreed to meet and greet the children, to speak briefly, and to allow them to ask him some questions. My sense was that, being new, he may have been expecting inquiries concerning life in Oxford, but what came out was no such thing.

'That bird over there," one girl asked, "the one with the book on its back. What's that all about?"

"And those people up in that window," another insisted. "Who are they?"

"Harriet will tell you all about them," the good man replied.

II

In the beginning all that we sought was a connection between school and university, so that one might offer an introduction, and if possible an incentive, to the other. But it soon became apparent that such enlightenment does not appear unaided, and in due course we began to ask ourselves if there was anything we could do to expedite the process. When I say 'we' I should add that nothing was without change, and that chaplains and head teachers both underwent the process of change as time went by.

Harriet was herself followed, after nine years, by another chaplain, who came for only two, during which the program stopped functioning. It had been running very well the year before, indeed Harriet's best years were the last few, when the program was moving towards having the students engage the children more directly, and on topics they could navigate together. In any case, it was almost a year before anyone discovered what had happened, and by that point he was disinclined to take it up again. He did undertake other literary projects, and taught English literature to visiting students from Sarah Lawrence College, while organizing a circle to read religious poetry together in the chaplaincy. He had too theological commitments, and in the interests of inclusion – since he believed it offended some students – removed the Apostles' Creed from Wadham's Evensong, a somewhat startling innovation that remains in place to this day. He in turn was followed by a most able young chaplain and scholar, who also stayed two years. Hebrew learning in early modern Britain was his field, one that I heard him make interesting and relevant, quite brilliantly, to a general audience. He both pursued his academic work with evident success, and also revivified the Hermitage program, to the delight of Zoe Howe, now the equally able Head Teacher there, whose interest in making her charges aware of life beyond Tower Hamlets I have mentioned already. The new chaplain understood what was needed, and it began again. He had kindly gone out of his way to invite me to lunch when I was in Oxford after his appointment, and though we never became friends, my sense was that he had the program where he believed it needed to be, and required no further advice. In any case, he made quite an important contribution to it by his somewhat minimalist approach to its administration. Partly because his predecessor had avoided it, the program had been mooted when his position was advertised, though from what I recall his own experience with such ventures had been limited. He therefore made it a practice in his first year to telephone Hermitage in advance of coming down (our usual practice in the past), and then to accompany the students, a circumstance that allowed him both to see what was involved and to get to know Zoe, who liked his arrangements and his students very much. It was during this time too that Abdul-Hayee, Gregory, Zoe and I began to discuss the problem that is at the heart of this book, the engagement of ethnic minority children with higher education, but for a variety of reasons, the chaplain was not able to join us in those discussions, which took place in London. But he did pursue the Hermitage program, and did so effectively, and with a minimum of fuss. Thus he demonstrated that it is not only possible, it is not inconvenient to organize and direct a program like Wadham's, even in the challenging context of Tower Hamlets. To do so requires a degree of effort certainly, some considered imagination, and above all attention to what one is about. But as we say in America, it is not rocket science either. Perhaps it would be best to call it a human science, even one of the humanities; a little interest can go a long way. In any event, in his second year the chaplain no longer accompanied his students to Hermitage; there was no need to do so.

But another problem soon presented itself, specifically a sense that the early introduction of the idea of a university to the Tower Hamlets children was not quite enough, and that we needed to consider what else might matter, and why. It was Zoe who gave impetus to our discussion, and her thinking had been informed in conversation with other Heads as well. But as we considered, it became apparent that the heart was as necessary as the head in any such undertaking, and that adventuring into new lands necessitated carrying old ones along as well, or at least some of them. Zoe understood the necessity of considering gender as well, and also the traps laid for it, and saw deeply into her children's hopes and agitations. Though she did not share their culture she did their aspirations, and no one spoke for them with greater insight.

Having mentioned the changes that took place in the Wadham program I should probably describe as well one other program that developed soon after, when Zoe's immediate predecessor at Hermitage, Abdul-Hayee Murshad, left for an appointment at a larger Tower Hamlets School, Bigland Green Primary School, not far from White Chapel High Street. I had known Abdul–Hayee since 1993, when we both arrived at Hermitage, he in a more senior and enduring position than my own. But in Easter Term 2009, while holding a visiting fellowship at Magdalene College, Cambridge, I learned that, having completed a year at OFSTED (the Office of Standards in Education, the office that oversees schools), he would like to introduce a similar program to Bigland Green. As things stood at the time, Magdalene had only a visiting chaplain, a former bishop who was disinclined to make any commitment that might devolve upon his successor, so I made inquiries with the chaplain at Clare College, already famous for its investment in such work, and the college whose remit included Tower Hamlets. Clare had been one of the first colleges to seek to attract state school students actively, having begun some years since with recruiting such children in years 11 and 12, at a time when many another college was looking the other way. More recently, I am told, the percentage of Clare students coming from state schools is the highest in Cambridge.

The Clare chaplain, actually called the Dean, whom I approached in June 2009 proved to be the Reverend Doctor Gregory Seach, a well-spoken, markedly perceptive and thoughtful Australian priest, who was fully attuned to what we understood the issues to be, and very willing to engage them. During our first conversation I made a point of mentioning that we worked with younger children, years 5 and 6, not 11 and 12, and he took the point at once. Those concerned with outreach at Clare had come to understand that if you were going to interest minority children in applying to university it was necessary to start young, he said, and that was what they were seeking to do. In short order we made arrangements to visit Abdul-Hayee.

I have mentioned Tower Hamlets so often now that I should probably say something about it, at least from the students' point of view. Reaching Hermitage was not difficult though from Oxford it took time, and until the very end of the trip the way there seemed to pass largely through tourists' London. Tower Hill was the tube stop, and the way from there wound through St Katherine's Dock, which may have welcomed impoverished Russian and Jewish refugees fleeing the Czar's pogroms in the nineteenth century, but was now more accustomed to what certainly looked like multi-million-pound yachts in the twenty-first. Bigland Green was longer and more difficult of access, but perhaps closer to the culture of the place, and one did not come away from it with the feeling that a wrong turn might lead to an encounter with Donald Trump.

Particularly in the early days of the program I would sometimes take students new to it on a little walking excursion into Whitechapel, away from the former warehouses now made into posh apartment buildings in Wapping, where the Hermitage School and Mr. Murdock's Times Newspapers so firmly stood. Our destination was Whitechapel High Street, reached through the Aldgate East tube stop, a varied and commercial delight in a neighborhood that, perhaps especially to an American eye, still carried visions of Jack the Ripper, and more happily, of the Elephant Man and his East London, now Royal, Hospital, which stands not far from the justly famous Whitechapel Art Gallery, and the Blind Beggar Pub, in which the infamous Kray brothers committed their last murder. Just off White Chapel runs Commercial Road, off which, in the late nineteenth century, a group of Oxford colleges established a few secular settlement houses, primarily so that their undergraduates might work with and instruct residents during the summer months. Over the years, over 100 different courses were offered to over 1,000 students. The best-known house was Balliol's, made famous as Toynbee Hall, and named after a recently deceased member of its Senior Common Room. It was constructed to look like the red brick entrance to the Oxford Union — even today the resemblance is striking. But the last institution remaining was Wadham House, which remained until 1918, and so stood as the last vestige of Oxford in the area, at least until a new Wadham program began at Hermitage School, on May Day, 2000.

To some or all of these attractions I introduced Wadham students in the early days of the program, on walks through the area, and indirectly to one other attraction as well, whose interest I had not fully understood at the time. Not far from the Whitechapel tube stop, just across the street from the East London Hospital, is an open-air street market that sells more or less everything, but clothes in particular. One cold November day (I think it was) I had taken a small group of students on the walk I have just described, and as we turned to return for cokes and pizza back at the Arts Café that Toynbee Hall had since become, one among them spotted a collection of surplus Army greatcoats, for sale at 5 pounds each, a real bargain, at the open air market. Looks were exchanged and decisions made. Wadham students were again in the East End, and by no means as tourists.

III

But with the entrance of Clare College into our narrative, and with Rev. Dr. Gregory Seach joining our group, we achieved a critical mass of persons interested in meeting together to discuss both the operation of our programs and the larger issue of how to connect able young students to a university, in such a way that they will engage with it when the time comes. As I have already said, for the last couple of years Abdul-Hayee, Gregory, Zoe and I met off and on in order to see how the Hermitage/Wadham, Bigland Green/Clare programs were progressing, and what we could do to improve and support them. But such was only part of our agenda, for we also would discuss how to preserve an interest in university beyond primary school. It was not at all an ideological position we sought, still less a political one. We understood it rather as an intellectual problem of importance to the education and the lives of the children concerned, one that needed to be addressed practically and not theoretically, and that might, one day at least, lead to resolution. We would invite others to our discussion, other teachers and administrators from the schools involved, and occasionally, as already reported, officers from Camden.

There were unexpected benefits to the association as well. It transpired, for example, that Clare had a fund that, when considered carefully, could allow for a donation to support the expansion of Bigland Green's library, and also for not one, but several trips to Clare from Bigland Green, not only by the children, but also by the staff, so that they too could understand the operation, and see what Cambridge had to offer. This did not happen at Wadham, and I doubt that it often happens elsewhere, but the simple act of bringing school staff to visit a university can have a happy effect both on the internal dynamic of the school, and on the ease with which the subject can be broached. It also helped to deepen the connection between Clare and Bigland Green School, so that in short order – or at least in two years – the connection between the two seemed as close as that between Hermitage and Wadhan. Yet both intermittently and especially as time went on, our discussions seemed to work best when the four of us talked together, asking effectively what had we learned, and what had we not. We understood, of course, that what we arrived at were not the only possible answers, indeed many of them remained questions still, toward whose answers we hoped to be moving. But then and all too suddenly it came to an end. Gregory was needed in Australia, it was time for me to return to Georgetown, and Wadham's new chaplain, after expressing interest initially, turned, as we shall see, to other things instead. So let me write here, toward the end of chapter four, what we considered we had learned.

Helping children actually understand the reason for higher education is not easily accomplished. But we considered that such understanding is actually a process, not a lesson, and one of no very great difficulty (except when it is), but one that touches a child's life at three points in particular. First, in Years 2 and 3, when a child is first getting to understand what school is all about, representations from slightly older children, in years 5 or 6 say, can help to broaden that understanding by saying what it was they learned during their day-trip to, for example, Oxford. Good teachers do not need Lev Vygotsky to tell them how effectively a slightly older child can instruct a younger one, and how powerful such instruction can become. Second, children in years 5 and 6 need to be engaged as their primary school years come to an end, and, in year 6 at least, as their secondary school years rise before them. Here too the practice of describing their university outing to their younger schoolmates is a good one, both for the opening it offers the very young, and also because of what is learned in teaching.

But the next stage was the one that most engaged us, and led to the longest discussions. For it speedily became apparent to us that whatever was accomplished in primary school could be undermined at a stroke in secondary, and more easily in the early years, when new friendships are formed and the reefs and shoals of early adolescence begin to appear before them. During this time too I began to read, somewhat randomly I must admit, but more extensively than since I had left Berkeley, in American Educational journals around issues encountered during the process of Middle School entrance, xeroxing first articles then abstracts, the latter of which I recall inflicting on Gregory. But what struck me most forcibly at the time was a concern, among many articles, to find a key that would effectively undo all locks, and work regardless of context. This was a concern that we, who kept our focus upon Tower Hamlets, never shared. One of the concerns that drove our discussion was the evident cultural differences posed by a specific and complex Muslim community, differences that had to be noted and respected, and not seen as an impediment to the task at hand. Gender was one of these, but other, often family attitudes, were relevant too, though our concern was less to identify and describe such attitudes, as to consider how they might contribute to the route to higher education for certain excellent young people who might otherwise not go there. But our focus was on both, and by no means did we discuss cultural difference only, nor did we promote its discussion as we might have. Our focus, rather, was practical and *ad rem*. What would or might lead in the right direction – and how would we get there? In many ways, Abdul-Hayee's connections in the community were of first importance, though Zoe's concern for the education of girls – a concern we all shared – was ever-present too. But we tried to fight shy of generalizations, and to legislate not *orbi*, and only somewhat *urbi*, but above all to be specific, not to claim the mantel of scholarship, but only that of pedagogy, since it was in the best interest of our children, not of ourselves, that we were working.

Thus issues of cultural difference were present in our discussions, which also involved, through Abdul-Hayee, the Head Teacher of Stepney Green Secondary School, which over the years had received very many students from Bigland Green and Hermitage Schools both. As we turned more and more to the first years after primary school, interaction with his school became of greater and greater interest, together with considerations as to how, or in what ways, connections could be made and kept. Those questions, however, remained finally unanswered, thought at least the necessity of asking them became apparent to us.

At this point, and after (believe me) further discussion, Clare rose, magnificently in my judgment, to the occasion, and agreed to allow a small group of year 8 and 9 school children from Stepney Green to come to the college for an overnight visit, together with a parent or another care-giver. The month selected was September, before the undergraduates returned, and sadly, all 15 of the students had to be male, thanks to the way the relevant laws and regulations were written – a circumstance that we all regretted very much. It was understood that, in many cases, the appropriate parent would be at least as likely to be female as male, whatever the gender of the pupil, since subsequent support and encouragement to stay on track was more likely to appear there. In the event, the visit was judged by all who took part in it to be a resounding, albeit incomplete, success. Parents, fellows and others conversed easily together both in interactions during the day and also in the evening, and issues of gender, preparation and custom were among those mooted. The understanding was that those concerned had addressed, not that they had resolved, a difficult issue, had taken a step forward, and begun to show where the challenge lay. We rather hoped, I suppose, that time would heed Vergil's plea, and be favorable to bold beginnings.

5

Concluding?

A Surprise at Wadham—the Good Chaplain—Cambridge to the Rescue —Outreach and the Very Young—Beginning Again—And Again?

I

Henry David Thoreau remarks that he left Walden for as good a reason as he went there, but he does not say what it was. Conjecture has turned around his increasing investment in the Abolitionist movement, and the inconvenience of having to travel to Boston and beyond from a cabin in the woods, but in some ways, and given the nature of the requirements he identified at Walden, he never really left it. Nor, I suppose, will Wadham, an eminently progressive college, entirely relinquish the program that connected it to Hermitage School, though the new chaplain, perhaps like Thoreau, was apparently ready to move on. On May 29, 2015, I came in to Wadhan for lunch with the new chaplain and two of her colleagues, to be told that early in the academic year the chaplain had effectively discontinued the program. No one had been told that that was so, not even Zoe, whom the chaplain had visited at Hermitage soon after her appointment, and to whom she had promised continuation.

Zoe had however asked for a delay until after OFSTED's soon expected visit (OFSTED is the Office of Standards in Education that oversees schools), and so the Chaplain insists that a call should have come when the visit was over. For some reason, never explained, she had not called back herself, though in the past the call had come from the college when the chaplain is ready to proceed. In any case, soon thereafter the chaplain had communicated with other teachers, some known to her, and offered them Wadham students for their classrooms. It's all for the best, I am told, and besides, whatever happened in the past, this group of Wadham students didn't want to travel as far away as London for only a day.

That representation reminded me later of a perspective I have already recalled, concerning the usefulness of engagement and exchange between the still young and the very young, especially when they come from different towns. Such discourse need not attach itself to attitudes or objects of culture as such; common parlance on most subjects is quite sufficient, if impossible to quantify. But it seems to be the testimony of these programs that academic exchange can offer encouragement to both parties. I was recently reminded of this circumstance by an early participant in the Sursum Corda program, one of the very few who went on to Georgetown, then, in his case, to a Masters degree at Johns Hopkins. Once, when we were rehearsing his career, he insisted that it was his ability to speak with and to those from whom he differed – to white people, he said – that made it possible for him to move and leap and parry as he had; and that he had learned from us, or at least with us. This was in contrast to a brother, who had chosen a different course.

Increasingly we separate ourselves, meet in passing, and are only intimate with those we recognize. By the time we understand our practice the hour has passed, and we have chosen one or two from out a multitude. Why accost someone I hardly know when I can oblige a friend? Why go to London when there are children enough in Oxford? But is not a university advantaged, even made excellent, by diversity? Is not a college? It is not only the university we champion, but also the sometimes difficult way there, and the unaccountable pleasure of talking over a divide. Or simply of talking, the language arts rejigged, and making of one another a different world. So again, when students talk to children what matters most is what they take for granted in the end.

In truth, different chaplains had managed or avoided the program in different ways. The previous chaplain had made it a practice to accompany his students when they went to Hermitage, and Harriet used to describe Hermitage as Wadham's "flagship" program, though later she also established a connection to a local school in Blackbird Leys. This had proved useful to Wadham students interested in continuing on in education, and wanting to develop pedagogical practices, and to test their commitment, before graduating.

There seemed to be a distinction among the chaplains, however, that may mean something or nothing. The three chaplains who best understood, practically and pedagogically, but also perhaps theologically, the issues that were involved in the program, all three held a D. Phil.; the other two not. No doubt it could have been otherwise. Someone personally committed to the issues involving cultural difference and assisting disadvantaged children could have embraced the project, whereas someone with a D.Phil. might have looked the other way. But Oxford, as always, is in the process of change, so that almost every new fellow now has a D. Phil. at the time of his or her appointment; it was not always so. But when a new chaplain doesn't have one, then he or she can easily miss the academic cues, or simply decide that they don't matter, and do as he or she pleases.

In some colleges there is no one to whom (as we say in America) he or she should report, or simply to offer advice, and that is not necessarily the advantage that it may sound. This kind of work, that crosses race and class, has its complications, and in complicated work a degree of social sophistication can be an advantage. Thus it is quite possible to listen to what is expected in an interview, and say "Yes, yes, I understand," but not to understand, and to go one's way. If there are Christians among the college's fellows, they may be disinclined to ask hard questions, and those uninterested in religious matters ditto, if for different reasons. The chaplain is particularly unencumbered, a friend tells me, if the Head of the SCR —of which, in Wadham, neither the Warden nor the Chaplain is a member—takes no interest. Could lead to some interesting situations.

After that eventful lunch nothing happened. I had almost five weeks left in my visit, and had taken care that those involved should know as much. But nothing followed, and it was evident that the academic year was effectively over, and that the only expectation was that I would soon be leaving. A fellow of the college whom I knew represented to the Chaplain and to the college outreach fellow "disappointment" at what had come to pass – but both denied that anything had – which was right in a way, since for about seven months nothing had.

But meanwhile Magdalene College, a Cambridge college that had long been considering such a program, came into the picture, and it became evident that, though founded not by a woman but by a Benedictine monk, it could assume Wadham's place. I hoped that the details of any subsequent agreement should be specified, in detail and in good English prose, and in due course that may come to pass; it hasn't yet, but something better has. A smart and perceptive Magdalene undergraduate, informed of the possibility by her college, became interested in seeing if she could, with others, develop a connection between Hermitage and Magdalene, and urged by me visited the school, took copious notes during a long conversation with Zoe, and undertook to do what she could. She was thought by all concerned to be both understanding and perceptive, and to offer the real promise of what public men refer to as a new beginning. Unlike many a student, she understood what it meant to be disadvantaged, recognized at once what the project sought to accomplish, and what, and how much, undergraduate students might reasonably undertake. And now it is 20 November 2015, and the first group of students from Magdalene has visited Hermitage, together with their new chaplain. The encounter could not have gone better, and after the seminar, the group turned a kind of generalized Q and A that we have used before into something more specific, in which each Clare student (and the Chaplain) responded to questions from a small group of children. It went so well that it bids fair to become part of the agenda. But in any case, it was time to start again.

II

Throughout this narrative I have not said much about the role of the university, except to notice that the sense is now, in both Oxford and Cambridge, that outreach is a college as much as a university matter. Further, the nation having been divided up among the colleges, the burden of recruiting state school students is increasingly on the colleges. This circumstance has led to a number of large and apparently welcoming programs, not only visits to colleges from secondary state schools, but among the more imaginative colleges, visits in reverse by some of the more enlightened fellows, who realize that it is not only students who can get caught up in the "bubble" that is a university, and that for outreach to be worthy of the name, connections should operate in both directions.

University visits by older schoolchildren may be helpful in making the institution less intimidating, or at least more familiar, an undertaking at least as necessary in America as in Britain, and anything that encourages the young to proceed has my vote. Still, there is a constitutional impersonality embedded in mass visits everywhere that can make them seem, even to those taking part, as intended primarily for the advantaged, who can move on to another "school" if refused at this one. Fall in Georgetown brings with it a myriad of "college visits," in which parents and high school Juniors and Seniors (years 11 and 12) come to be lectured to and led about campus by well-instructed undergraduates so as to help them decide whether Georgetown is worth the wick. Like many another university, Georgetown insists that it practices "needs blind admission," but four years with us costs roughly two hundred thousand dollars, which is why parents come as well. For that reason among others, everyone tends to be attentive, but the smart question is Will my child be happy here? Sadly, not all who think so will be admitted.

In Oxford, the students who attend "Open Days" seem at once more enthusiastic and more fragile than their American counterparts, and are usually on their mettle, if deferential in a way that ours have not yet learned. The children I have been writing about, or some of them, will one day be those students, with their gentleness and their abandon, but to encourage those who are truly other you must go deeper, and know them for more than a day. Thus, if you are concerned to embrace black and brown students as well as white, to encourage them to enter higher education whether for the intrinsic value of the experience, or to improve their futures, new ways may be needed. To be sure, circumstance sets limits. But children grow to what they understand. And they learn from one another best of all.

The problems, of course, hardly end there. Left to their own devices, the young, but not only the young, will invariably invent their own world, and fill it with language of their own. One other challenge that America shares with Britain concerns the development of new regional dialects – in London today, and also in Miami, Florida, in Sacramento, California, and places in between -- that the disadvantaged are weaving together, made up of the web of languages and dialects among which they live. In Miami the mixing of Spanish and English is now so common that in many places they blend together seamlessly, without any consciousness that a hybrid is present, and with scant attention to tense. "*Veniste el somer?,*" my student is asked in Miami, where the practice is wide spread, by someone wanting to know if he will return in July. But he easily understands what is being asked, and replies at once. In Sacramento, the story goes, the police discovered that they could not communicate with a group of young bank robbers whom they had trapped in a bank, because they spoke no known language, only one invented among themselves, out of Spanish, Hmong, English and Vietnamese. In London young men are embarked on a similar linguistic adventure, mixing languages so as to stay together closely, but gradually losing contact with whatever had come before, and limiting their futures and their lives. Meeting students can help with that, if only a little.

An inability to communicate across cultural boundaries can take other forms as well. Increasingly, British colleges are hiring students the year after graduation to oversee or direct their "outreach program." The salaries are not large, but the power is real, and one doesn't have to move. Still, the order and organization they bring is unconnected with programs like the ones I have been describing, and for the most part is concerned with years 11 and 12. The outreach officer is concerned with thousands, not with a particular school that wants more than its due, or seem to. So emails go unanswered; no students visit; a common grayness colors everything. The Head Teacher at the neglected school, older and aware of what is going on, remains polite, tries not to be offended. And if there are issues of race involved, things deepen all around. The young can not be told to be sensitive, because they believe that they already are. Some more than others, no doubt. But the power is real, and they are grown-ups now.

Still, among school children, and with those beginning secondary school, it is altogether appropriate to begin to reach out. Some seem to require a separate structure, one that can be understood and agreed to from the beginning. Individual colleges still matter in Oxford, where the D.Phil. is now king, and is it such a bad thing that your book matters more than your college's place on the Norrington Table? In Georgetown, our Provost blogs about research and publication, but not about teaching, which has no effect on the university's designation as a Research-1 (R-1) university. Are there thus educational practices, possibly American in origin, in which person matters less than quantity? Is it true that a minister of education once expressed surprise that anyone would want to study medieval history – which he thought the state shouldn't support? And is it actually possible that the Britain of Beowulf, Chaucer and yes, Shakespeare, proposes NO money for graduate research in the humanities next year? And if so, where are the much deservèd protests?

Throughout, I have sometimes used the word "disadvantaged" in reference to the children whom we sought to serve. The word does not lend itself to much elaboration, nor is it, in this context, easy to define. The British children among whom we work are bright, perceptive, and loving. Their parents love and esteem them, and far more of them live in nuclear families than the children with whom I work in Washington, D.C. But somehow, for all of that, they live apart, and if this book has one theme, one secret, it is that one.

I saw this for the first time more than a decade ago, but then again more recently. As we have already seen, when the children from Hermitage arrived at Wadham on their return visit, an expedition that used to be carried out by bus but later by train, they were allowed to run about in the fellows' garden for a time, to stretch their legs after three hours travelling. The garden has within it a variety of old trees, many large, and one in particular, sadly since fallen and removed, towered above the rest. It was these trees, however, more than anything else, that immediately attracted the children, accustomed as they were to the hard open areas, and the new, thin trees of Tower Hamlets.

"Look at the huge trees," one boy called out excitedly to the others when he first saw them, stopping in his tracks, here in the middle of Oxford. "There are really lots of them. Come and see. Hurry."

Photo Gallery

For several years the American photographer Harry Mattison worked with the residents of the Washington, D.C. community known as Sursum Corda as a friend and collaborator, recording and helping with autobiographies, and forming a photographic record of the community as a whole. Aware that the Sursum Corda program is the only one treated here that is not attached to a particular school, we have, with Mr. Mattison's permission, printed a small selection from this rich archive, focusing primarily on the children and the architecture of the Sursum Corda community.

www.ingramcontent.com/pod-product-compliance
Lightning Source LLC
Chambersburg PA
CBHW031644170426
43195CB00035B/569